The Power of the Blood of Jesus Christ

"God Wants Everyone to Go to Heaven"

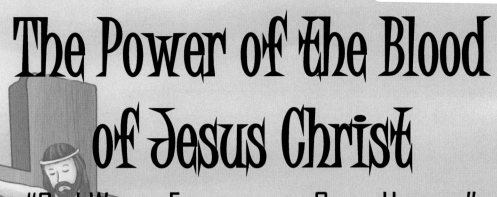

The Power of the Blood of Jesus Christ

"God Wants Everyone to Go to Heaven"

Izabella Cooper

& Dr. Caleb Cooper

Illustrated by: Afzal Khan

To order products, or for any other correspondence:
Hunter Heart Kids™ A Division of Hunter Entertainment Network™
Colorado Springs, Colorado 80840
www.hunter-ent-net.com
Tel. (253) 906-2160
E-mail: contact@hunter-entertainment.com
Or reach us on Facebook or Instagram at: Hunter Entertainment Network
"Offering God's Heart to Kids All Over the World"

This book and all other Hunter Entertainment Network™ Hunter Heart Publishing™, and Hunter
Heart Kids™ books are available at Christian bookstores and distributors worldwide.

Chief Editor: Deborah G. Hunter
Book cover design/Illustrator: Phil Coles Independent Design/Afzal Khan
Layout & logos: Exousia Marketing Group www.exousiamg.com
ISBN (Paperback): 9798549424913
Library of Congress Control Number: 2022906391

For Worldwide Distribution, Printed in the United States of America

ABOUT THE AUTHOR

Izabella Cooper

My name is Izabella Cooper, and I am 8 years old. I love Jesus. I like to worship and pray. I want to learn how to play the piano. I like to sing songs about Jesus. I believe God is good all the time, and helps me when I need Him the most. I believe that Jesus died on the cross and shed His blood for our sins.

I like to spend time with my family. I like to ride my bike. I like to play with my cute baby dolls.

DEDICATION

FIRST AND FOREMOST
JESUS CHRIST GETS ALL THE GLORY FOR THIS BOOK!

Thank you, Erica Cooper who has been anointed by God to daily teach Izabella and her brother Caleb Titus Cooper. She has made many sacrifices in life to commit herself to full-time homeschooling, raising both children in the admonition of the Lord! Her consistent Godly training and equipping through homeschooling has laid a strong foundation for this children's book and more books to come.

FOREWORD

Although I love seeing people of all ages being touched by the power of God, there is truly nothing more pure or beautiful than seeing a child going after the Lord. During *The Brownsville Revival*, I had the honor of witnessing hundreds of children on their knees under the glory of the Lord.

My prayer is that we will see a generation of children encountering the true and authentic love of Jesus that will spread across the world! May their genuine hearts spark a desire in teenagers and adults to go after Jesus like never before!

I love seeing precious Izabella Cooper using her voice to worship the Lord—her love for Jesus is authentic and her love for people is evident in her tender yet bold personality. I pray the Lord continues to raise her up for His glory!

Jeri Hill
The Wife of the Late Steve Hill of the Great Brownsville Revival
Togetherintheharvest.com

Acts 2:22-24

"Men of Israel, hear these words: Jesus of Nazareth, a man attested by God to you by miracles, wonders, and signs which God did through Him in your midst, as you yourselves also know. Him, being delivered by the determined purpose and foreknowledge of God, you have taken by lawless hands, have crucified and put to death; whose God raised up, having loosed the pains of death, because it was not possible that He should be held by it."

Jesus is great, mighty, and powerful. He loves and protects everybody. Jesus created everybody in His own image. This means that He created you in His own image, and He loves you and will protect you, too. Jesus will save you from your sins, and your family's sins, in this life.

Have your parents ever asked you to clean your room and you said, "No"? Did you know that when you say no to them that you are disobeying your parents and God?

Have you ever talked back to your parents in a bad way?
This is another way that sin works.

Have you ever told your parents "no" when they asked you to go to your room because you were grounded? This is another way that sin works in a kid's life.

4

As you can see, all of us have disobeyed God in different ways. This means we need the power of the blood of Jesus Christ to help us.

Did you know that Jesus can save you from your sins?
God loves His people so much that He sent His only begotten Son
to die on the cross to save people from the pit of hell.

6

Hell is the worst place that you can be. You can get there by not receiving the blessing of Jesus Christ. If you want to be saved, you have to receive the blood of Jesus Christ.

Jesus Christ was nailed in His hands and His feet on the Cross of Calvary. When they nailed Him, His blood spilt on the land, so that everybody could receive His blood.

8

The power of the blood of Jesus can change people's lives forever. Have you ever received the blood of Jesus Christ?

When you receive the blood of Jesus, Heaven opens up to you. When Jesus comes back on a beautiful white horse, you will go to Heaven because you received the blood of Jesus.

If you receive the blood of Jesus before you die and before Jesus comes back, then you will still go to Heaven before He comes back for those who received Jesus.

11

Jesus died on the Cross of Calvary. They took Him off the cross and put Him in a tomb. Then, the people thought that Jesus died for good.

But on the third day, Jesus resurrected, and He lived again. If Jesus defeated death, then we can defeat death, too, but only by His Blood can we live again in Heaven.

Would you like to go to Heaven? Would you like for your family to go to Heaven? Then, you must receive the Blood of Jesus that was shed for us.

Pray this prayer with me:

Dear Heavenly Father, I want to invite You to come into my heart. I want Your precious blood that You shed for me. I repent for every wrong thing and every sin that tried to get in me and my family's life. Help me to be more Godly, because I want to go to Heaven when You come back for me and my family.

In Jesus' Name, Amen.

KID'S REVIVAL PRAYERS

A PRAYER FOR MY MOMMY

Jesus, I rise up and call my mommy blessed. Please be with my mommy and keep her safe in all that she does today. Give her strength in her body as she willingly works with her hands to make sure our family has all the yummy food our tummies need, clean clothes for our bodies and a nice, clean, and safe home to live and play in. Should her arms ever get tired, may she always find her strength in You, Jesus. Fill her to overflowing with the Holy Spirit and fire and may she walk everyday with You ever so closely. In Jesus' Name, Amen.

Erica Cooper
Izabella's Mommy/Pastor's Wife of New Hope Revival Church
Truth or Consequences, New Mexico

JESUS, BE WITH MY DADDY

Dear Daddy God, Daddy's are big, Daddy's are strong. There are still days when things go wrong. I pray my daddy will have strength from above. God give him what he needs to soar like a dove. When evil comes and tries to get near, send Holy Spirit to keep him from fear. Bless him and guide him at work every day. Go with him and give him the words he should say. Help him to always come home without fussing, enjoying his family and happy to see us. In Jesus' Name, Amen.

Dr. Caleb Cooper
Izabella's Daddy/Pastor of New Hope Revival Church
Truth or Consequences, New Mexico

LORD, FILL ME WITH HOLY SPIRIT

Dear Father God, thank You for being my friend, my Savior, and my Lord! Fill me with Your precious Holy Spirit, so that I can be useful for You and help to bring Your Kingdom to the earth, in Jesus' name! Lord, let me experience the fire of the Holy Spirit as You poured out at Azusa Street! Lord, I want to see Your glory, I have heard Your glory was seen at Azusa Street by many kids. Thank You, Lord, for leading and guiding me, and showing me Your glory. In Jesus' Name, Amen.

"Now when the apostles which were at Jerusalem heard that Samaria had received the word of God, they sent unto them Peter and John: Who, when they were come down, prayed for them, that they might receive the Holy Ghost: Then laid they their hands on them, and they received the Holy Ghost." (Acts 8:14-15, 17)

Apostles Fred & Wilma Berry
Azusa Street Mission
312 Azusa Street Los Angeles, California
azsusastreetmission.org

LORD, TEACH ME YOUR WAYS

Dear God, Thank You for being so good to me. Thank You for sending Jesus to take away my sins. Thank You for sending the Holy Spirit to touch my heart when I do something wrong, so that I can repent. Thank You for giving me my prayer language, so I can talk to You in a special and powerful way. Lord, please keep teaching me to know You and how You do things, so I can show my friends Your love. Lead me to someone to tell about You today. In Jesus' Name, Amen.

LaNora Morin
Gilbert, Arizona
FountainGate Ministries International
fountaingateintl.org
fgsor.org

LORD, KEEP ME HOLY!

Dear Father, Set me on fire for Your Word and through Your Spirit, so I can live HOLY for Jesus all the days of my life. Guard me, shield me, and protect me from the evil of this world. Create in me a clean heart and renew a right spirit within me. May purity be my banner and wisdom spring forth out of my belly. I don't want to be lukewarm, but I want to be on HOLY FIRE for the Kingdom of God! Use me, Oh Lord, for Your glory and set my generation on fire that we may destroy the darkness and evil in this world with Your power. Let my love and fire for You spread everywhere the soles of my feet touch. Let me be a HOLY example of Your keeping power to my friends, and to this next generation. In Jesus' Name, Amen.

Deborah G. Hunter
Colorado Springs, Colorado
Publisher/ Hunter Entertainment Network
Author: Holy Spirit: The Promise Left for the Believer

JESUS, HELP THOSE IN NEED

Dear Lord, I see so many people in the streets wanting food, I pray that you move on them and save them, so they could be good people and they can help others. I pray for those out of town and people living here, touch their hearts so they can worship you every day. I worship you, I praise your name, You made everything in the whole world, and I know that you can do everything, You can move mountains, Please Lord Keep my family safe all the time, put Angels to guard us, on each one of us my family and my friends, Thank You Lord. In Jesus' Name, Amen.

Ron and Tyda Harvey
CEO of Gathering of Tribal Nations
Harvest Time Network Ministry
Window Rock, Arizona-Navajo Nation
www.htnm.org

NOTHING IS IMPOSSIBLE WITH GOD

Dear Jesus, I pray for my mom, my dad, my brothers, and my sisters. Jesus, please help them and keep them safe and sound, nothing is impossible with You. I put them in Your hands, I know that You will answer my prayer. You are so awesome Lord, and I love You with my whole heart. In Jesus' Name, Amen.

Jerry Tom
Pastor of Window Rock Christian Center
Window Rock, Arizona-Navajo Nation
windowrockcc.org

BURNING BRIGHT WITH HOLY FIRE

Heavenly Father, From the top of my head to the bottoms of my feet, let Your Holy Fire Burn bright inside of me, Ignite my soul with fierce fire from above as I speak in thy Holy Tongues and Prophesy of Your great love. May I roar like a lion in fierce praise unto You. Baptize all the children of the world to burn as "Holy Flames" for You. In Jesus' Name, Amen.

Frances Alvarez
Open Door Ministries
Bisbee, Arizona

JESUS, PLEASE SEND ME

Before I lay me down to sleep, there is something still that makes me weep. My heart, my heart, in such alarm, because so many don't know Your arms. Bunches, and bunches like sheep astray, they aren't ready for Judgement Day. Lord, I feel so weak, I feel so small. I need Your help to reach them all! You're a big, big God, and I'm just me, yet tonight I pray You find Your sheep, and if I can help, Lord, please send me! In Jesus' Name, Amen.

Evangelist Levi Lutz
Together In The Harvest Ministries
Orlando, Florida
Togetherintheharvest.com

KID'S FAITH TO SEE AND HEAR

God, I love You very much. I want Jesus to live in my heart. I want to see with "faith eyes," and hear with "faith ears," and "do what is right and what is good." I want to show others God's heart by loving and praying for them and believing God can use me to do good works and see miracles that will change their lives. I want to learn all about Jesus, so I can be like Him and show His power to others because He is living in my heart. God, You said that unless all people become as a little child, we cannot "receive" the Kingdom of God (Matthew 10:15). God, help all people to have the faith and belief of a child because we can be used by You to bring Heaven to Earth. In Jesus' Name, Amen.

Sandy Segura
Heartland Apostolic Prayer Network
Albuquerque, New Mexico

20

PRAISING GOD AS HE LEADS ME

Father God, Thank You for Your goodness. Thank You for Your unending kindness. Thank You for Your perfect love that will never let go of me. Please fill me with Your Holy Spirit every day and teach me Your ways. Give me wisdom and discernment to navigate every day in a way that honors You. Help me honor my parents, too. Let me be a bright shining light in my community that leads people directly to You! In Jesus' Name, Amen.

Devonna Denee Reyes
Santa Fe, New Mexico
Breath.pray.worship.love@gmail.com

JESUS, DRAW ME CLOSE TO YOU

Father, I pray that You move by Your Spirit and draw us SO close to You. Thank You, Jesus, for giving Your life for us, so that we could receive forgiveness. Thank You for sending Holy Spirit to give us strength and power to live in victory for you. Have your way in my life. In Jesus' Name, Amen.

Jeri Hill
Orlando, Florida
The Wife of the Late Steve Hill of the Great Brownsville Revival
Togetherintheharvest.com

JESUS INSIDE OF ME

Dear Lord, pour out Your Holy Spirit onto us like a mighty flood and wash us in Your blood. Purify our hearts and minds, so that Your Word is the truest word we find. May we learn to seek Your will; even when things are messy, help our heart to be still. Your perfect plan and purpose will come to light, for You will help us to shine so very bright. Draw each of us closer to You, to be the light of the world that shines even brighter than a July fourth view. Be a lamp upon our feet to show us Your desires and away from the devil's defeat. For we can do all things through You Lord, for You chose me and it's me You love and adore. We are warriors in Your strength; Lord, we will not be worriers. You paid the ultimate sacrifice, so it's Your glory that will be magnified. Carve us in Your image and set our hearts afire, so that others we may inspire. May our only desire be to lift Your name and Your glory. Oh Lord, burn inside of us like a flame. Thank You for Your grace, each and every day, it's Your name that we embrace! In Jesus' Name, Amen.

Jazmine S. Hall
Children's Church Pastor of New Hope Revival Church
Truth or Consequences, New Mexico

I AM THE NEXT REVIVAL GENERATION

*Father, we know we are the generation where the fire **must not** go out for the great harvest of Revival is still yet to come and is taking place right now! We speak fire to fall down on earth as it did at Pentecost and we don't stop there, we ask for MORE of You. Generations before and behind us will be touched by the same fire that is coming in our midst! Look! God, my hands are clean, my heart is pure just like Psalm 24:4! You said in Psalm 24:5: We shall receive the blessing from You, and righteousness from You of your salvation. We believe Psalms 24:6-8 is happening through us right now! "This is the generation of them that seek Him, that seek thy face, Selah. Lift up your heads, o ye gates; and be ye lift up, ye everlasting doors; and the King of glory shall come in. Who is this King of glory? The Lord strong and mighty, the Lord mighty in battle." You are the King of Glory that we make space for You to invade!*

We know because of Proverbs 29:18, "Where there is no vision, the people will perish." Prepare this generation I'm in Jesus for visions, revelations, and Your burning love for us to blaze a trail upon this uttermost LIFE, leading us to the mighty outpouring! The fiery love of Revival IS coming! Pour it out, Holy Spirit we pray! In Jesus' Name, Amen.

Sarah Hampton
Tulsa, Oklahoma

23

THANKFUL FOR WHO GOD IS AND ALL THAT HE HAS DONE

Dear Daddy God, Today, I am thankful for my mom, dad, and for all my loved ones who are such a blessing in my life. Thank You for our home, our car, our clothes, and my toys. Every good gift comes from You, "The Father of Lights." Thank You for the first breath I breathed when I awoke this morning, to the beautiful warm sunshine and the pretty birds that sang their songs. Lord, help me to always see the beauty and the good in all things. Help me to have gratitude in my heart each and every day, remembering to thank You. More than anything, to thank You for Jesus and Him dying on the cross for all of us, so we could all be together with You one day.

Thank You, Jesus, for Your love that caused You to suffer and bleed for our sins on that cross. Nailed and hanging on that cross with Your arms wide open, You were saying, "I Love You This Much!" In Jesus' Name, Amen. Psalm 118 says, "Give thanks to the Lord, for He is good; His love endures forever."

Elsa Thompson-Fallstich
Silver City, New Mexico

EVERYDAY BELONGS TO JESUS

Good Morning Jesus, I pray today that Heaven opens, You have lots to say. You are God, there is nothing You can't do. I'm a little kid that can do big things, too. My heart is Yours to do as You will. Fill me with Your presence and become so real to me. This life I live is not my own; I want to be like Jesus before I'm grown. Every day, before my day gets away, may Holy Spirit prepare my way. God, show me when I do wrong, I'll ask for forgiveness and won't take too long. May this day be filled with lots of power Jesus, Your name is like a strong tower. God, teach me how to read my Bible everywhere I go. I want to bring Revival! In Jesus' Name, Amen.

Dr. Caleb Cooper
Pastor of New Hope Revival Church
Truth or Consequences, New Mexico

Resources for Parents: Author of: *Pioneering Prophetic Patterns of Purpose, Jesus Focused: Awakening Endtime Prophetic Strategy, The Call for Strong Godly Leadership: A Compilation of Leaders from the Church, Marketplace and Law Enforcement, The Convergence of Revival and the King's Arrival, and* Contributing Author in *Igniting Revival Fire Everyday.* Available at calebcooperministries.com and amazon.com.